Mysteries of the Silent Brotherhood of the East

Literature for

The Moorish Science

Temple of America

This Text is the Property of

_____

The Red Book

© 2014
Califa Media ™

Originally published by the
Moorish Science Temple of America

Authorized by
Grand Sheik Bro. Rami Abdullah Salaam El
I.A.H.H.T.

Prepared for Publication by
Sis. Tauheedah S. Najee-Ullah El

Sincerity

© 2014
Califa Media ™

Originally published by the
Moorish Science Temple of America

Authorized by
Grand Sheik Bro. Rami Abdullah Salaam El
I.A.H.H.T.

Prepared for Publication by
Sis. Tauheedah S. Najee-Ullah El

TABLE OF CONTENTS

About This Text	i.
Editors Note	ii.
Chapter I Life and Works of Jesus in Egypt and India	1
Chapter II Life Works of Jesus in Joseph's Home at the Age of Seven Years	2
Chapter III The Life and Works of Jesus at the Age of Ten Years	4
Chapter IV Jesus Talks with the Rabbi of the Ten Commands	6
Chapter V Jesus Again: His First Year of Divine Ministry	8
Chapter VI Jesus Presented with His Camel, Goes to Lahore Where He Abides	10
Chapter VII Again Elihu's lessons - The Mysteries of Egypt	12
Chapter VIII The Council of the Seven of the World	13
Chapter IX Opening Address of Jesus with the Seven Sages - Seven Days Silence	15
Chapter X Meeting of the Seven Sages to Make Laws for the Coming Age for the	17

TABLE OF CONTENTS

Chapter XI Jesus Reveals the Marriage Law of Man and Wife from Allah	19
Chapter XII Jesus Explains to Kaspar the Meaning of Silence and the Wisdom of Allah	21
Chapter XIII Jesus's Holy Answer to Lamaas	23
Chapter XIV Jesus Receives the Mystic Name and Number and Passed the	25
Chapter XV Jesus Passes the Second Brother-hood Test - Justice	27
Chapter XVI Jesus Passes the Third Brother-hood Test - FAITH	29
Chapter XVII Jesus Passes the Fourth Brother-hood Test; Takes the Fourth Degree of Adept	31
Chapter XVIII Jesus Passes the Fifth Adept Degree - Heroism	33
Chapter XIX Jesus Takes the Sixth Degree and Passed the Sixth Adept	35
Chapter XX The Adept Chamber of the Dead. The Mysteries of Egypt.	38
Chapter XXI Jesus, The Prophet Had Finished His Tasks, and Must Now Go to	40

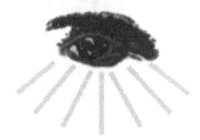

TABLE OF CONTENTS

Chapter XXII Jesus, The Prophet Had Finished His Tasks, and Must Now Go to the Sons of Men with Love Divine and Peace on Earth	41
Chapter XXIII Jesus Received the News of His Father's Death. Writes a Letter to His Mother	43

About This Text

12. The words of Buddha are recorded in the Indian sacred books. Attendeth them for they are part of the instructions of the Holy Breath.

13. The land of Egypt is the land of secret things.

14. The mysteries of the sages lie lock-bound in our Temples and Shrines.

15. The masters of all times and climes come here to learn. And when your sons have grown to manhood, they will finish all their studies in Egyptian schools.

16. But I have said enough. Tomorrow at the rising of the sun, we meet again.

The Red Book, Chapter VII

Grand Sheik, Brother Rami Salaam El is the head of the International Asiatic Hip Hop Temple and Managing Editor of the Moorning Star Newsletter. Bro. Salaam has extensive research experience, the demand for which has had led to travels around the world An avid student and teacher of contemporary Moorish American history. G.S. Salaam El lives in California.

Sister Tauheedah S. Najee-Ullah El was born into and educated by the Nation of Islam, Mosque Maryam in Chicago, Illinois. During her travels across America, she was led to the knowledge of her Moorish American nationality through the teachings of Noble Prophet Drew Ali. Sis. Najee-Ullah El is the Managing Editor of Califa Media & Califa Media-Canaanland. Sis. Najee-Ullah El travels extensively, and at the time of original, lives in California.

Additional Note

How to use this guide.

So that you may make most effective use of the instructions contained in this guide, I encourage the reader to have close at hand the following:

- A good standard dictionary of the English language, preferably one printed before 1965. The reason for this suggestion are two-fold: First, the book you hold is revised from a text originally published in 1928. Some of the words contained herein may no longer be in common use and/ or may have a different definition in modern dictionaries. Second, I suggest using a dictionary of this sort as many definitions—especially those pertaining to our people—were altered after the Civil Rights Movement in the United States. An example would be comparing the definitions of "American" in a pre-1965 dictionary versus one printed more recently.

  - Please note, there is no glossary contained in this guide to encourage use of the dictionary. Man—nor woman— knows not by being told.

- A Concordance of the Bible. As stated above, not all words are used correctly in these days and times. Additionally, words as used in the Bible should not be assumed to be the same used in common conversation.

- A Holy Quran of Mecca. The Prophet Noble Drew Ali did not release the Holy Koran of the Moorish Science Temple of America Circle Seven until between 1926 and 1928. The Moorish Holy Temple of Science, predecessor of the Moorish Science Temple of America, was founded in 1913 (Key 9). One must therefore ask themselves, what was the Prophet teaching from prior to the release of the Circle 7? Use of the Holy Quran of Mecca is further validated by its reference on our M.S.T. of A. Nationality Card: *"I do hereby declare that you are a Moslem under the divine Laws of the Holy Koran of Mecca..."*

- A bible of your choice. As you read this guide you will notice spaces to the exterior of the pages. These are reserved for any notes you may wish to make. Scholarly works encourage the student to make notes next to the item being noted for quick reference in the future.

Willing you much success in you endeavor to improve yourself, and thereby, our Nation,

Peace & Love

Sis. Tauheedah S. Najee-Ullah El

Chapter I

Life and Works of Jesus in Egypt and India

1. And Jesus came to Egypt Land and all was well. He tarried not upon the coast; he went at once to Zoan, home of Elihu and Salome, who five and twenty years before, had taught his mother in their sacred school.

2. And there was joy when met these three. When last the son of Mary saw these sacred groves, he was a babe.

3. And now, a man had grown strong by buffetings of every kind, a teacher who had stirred the multitudes in many lands.

4. And Jesus told the aged teachers all about his life, about his journey in foreign lands, about the meetings with masters, and about his kind receptions by the multitudes.

5. Elihu and Salome hears this story with delight; they lifted up their eyes to heaven and said"

6. "Our Father Allah, let now thy servants go in peace; for we have seen the glory of the Lord"

7. "And we have talked with him the messenger of Love and of the Covenant of Peace on earth and good will to men."

8. "Through Him shall all the Nations of the earth be blessed through Him, Immanuel."

9. And Jesus stayed in Zoan many days; and then he went forth unto the City of the Sun, that men call Heliopolis, and sought admission to the Temple of the sacred Brotherhood.

10. The council of the brotherhood convened, and Jesus stood before the hierophant. He answered all the questions that were asked with clearness and with power.

11. The hierophant exclaimed, "Rabboni of the rabbinate, why come you here? Your wisdom is the wisdom of the gods; why seek for wisdom in the halls of man?"

12. And Jesus said, "In every way of earth-life I would walk; in every hall of learning I would sit; the height that any man has gained, these I would gain;"

13. "What any man has suffered, I would meet; that I may know the griefs, the disappointments and sore temptations of my brother man, that I may know just how to succor with those in need."

14. "I pray you brothers, let me go into your dismal crypts; I would pass the hardest of your tests."

15. The master said, "Take then the vow of secret brotherhood;" and Jesus took the vow of secret brotherhood.

16. Again the master spoke, he said, "The greatest heights are gained by those who reach the greatest depths; and you shall reach the greatest depths."

17. The guide then led the way; and in the fountain Jesus bathed. And when he had been clothed in proper garb, he stood again before the hierophant.

Chapter II

Life Works of Jesus in Joseph's Home at the Age of Seven Years

1. The home of Joseph was on Marmion Way in Nazareth. Here Mary taught her son the lessons of Elihu and Salome;

2. And Jesus greatly loved the Vedic Hymns and the Avesta; but more than all he loved to read the Psalms of David and the pungent words of Solomon.

3. The Jewish books of prophecy were his delight; and when he reached his seventh year, he needed not the books to read; for he had fixed in memory every word.

4. Joachim and his wife, grand-parents of Jesus, made a feast in honor of the child; and all their near of kin were guests.

5. And Jesus stood before the guests and said, "I had a dream, and in my dream, I stood before the sea upon a sandy beach;"

6. "The waves upon the sea were high; a storm was raging on the deep."

7. "Someone above gave me a wand. I took the wand and touched the sands, and every grain of sand became a living thing. The beach was all a mass of beauty and song."

8. "I touched the waters at my feet, and they were changed to trees, and flowers and singing birds; and everything was praising Allah."

9. "And someone spoke. I did not see the one who spoke; I heard the voice, which said, 'There is no death.'"

10. Grandmother Ann loved the child. She laid her hand on Jesus's head and said, "I saw you stand beside the sea; I saw you touch the sand; and the waves, I saw them turn to living things; and then I knew the meaning of the dream"

11. "The sea of life rolls high; the storms are great; the multitude of men are idle, listless, waiting like dead sands upon the beach."

12. "Your want is Truth; with this you touch the multitude, and every man becomes a messenger of Holy light and life."

13. "You touch the waves upon the sea of life, their turmoils cease; the very winds become a song of praise."

14. "There is no death; because the wand of Truth can change the driest bones to living things, and bring the loveliest flowers from stagnant ponds, and turn the most discordant notes to harmony and praise."

15. Joachim said, "My son, today you pass the seventh milestone of your way of life; for you are seven years of age,

and we will give to you as a remembrance of this day whatever you desire. Choose that which will afford you most delight."

16. And Jesus said, "I do not want a gift, for I am satisfied. If I could make a multitude of children glad upon this day, I would be greatly pleased."

17. "Now there are many hungry boys and girls in Nazareth who would be pleased to eat with us, at this feast, and share with us the pleasures of this day."

18. "The richest gift that you can give to me is your permission to go out and find those needy ones, and bring them here that they may feast with us."

19. Joachim said, "Tis well. Go out and find the needy boys and girls, and bring them here. We will prepare enough for all."

20. And Jesus did not wait. He ran. He entered every home and hut and den of the town. He did not waste his words; he told his mission everywhere.

21. And in a little time one hundred and three score of happy children were following Jesus on Marmion way.

22. The guests made way; the banquet hall was filled with Jesus's guests; and Jesus and his mother served.

23. And there was food enough for all, and all were glad. So the birthday gift of Jesus was a crown of righteousness.

Chapter III

The Life and Works of Jesus at the Age of Ten Years

1. The great feast of Jews was on; and Joseph, Mary and their son, and many of their kin, went to Jerusalem. The child was ten years old.

2. And Jesus watched the butchers kill the lambs and birds and burn them on the altar in the name of Allah.

3. His tender heart was shocked at this display of cruelty. He asked the serving priest, "What is the purpose of this slaughter of the beasts and birds - why do you burn their flesh before Allah?"

4. The priest replied, "This is our sacrifice for sin. Allah has commanded us to do these things, and said, that in sacrifices all our sins are blotted out."

5. And Jesus said, "Will you be kind enough to tell when Allah proclaimed that sins are blotted out by sacrifices of any kind?"

6. "Did not David say that Allah requires not a sacrifice for sin? That it is sin itself to bring before His face burnt offerings for sin? Did not Isaiah say the same?"

7. The priest replied, "My child, you are beside yourself. Do you know more about the law of Allah than all of Israel? This is no place for boys to show their wit."

8. But Jesus heeded not his taunts; he went at once to Hillel and said to him,

9. "Rabboni, I would like to talk with you. I am disturbed about this service. I thought the Temple was the house of Allah; where Love and Kindness dwell."

10. "Do you not hear the bleating of those lambs; the pleading of those doves that men are killing over there? Do you not smell the awful stench of burning flesh?"

11. "Can you be kind and just, and still be filled with cruelty?"

12. "An Allah that takes delight in burning flesh and blood is not Allah of Love; he is not my Father."

13. "I want to find the Allah of Love; and, you, my master, you are wise; and surely you can tell me where to find the Allah of Love."

14. But Hillel could not give an answer to the child. His heart was stirred with sympathy. He called the child to him. He laid his hand upon his head and wept.

15. He said, "There is an Allah of Love; and you shall come with me, and, hand in hand, we will go forth and find Allah of Love."

16. And Jesus said, "Why need we go? I thought Allah was everywhere. Can we not purify our hearts and drive out cruelty and every wicked thought and make a Temple where Allah of Love can dwell?"

17. The master of the great courts felt as though he was himself a child; and that before him stood the master of all the laws.

18. He said within himself, "This child is surely a Prophet sent of Allah."

19. Then Hillel sought the parents of the child, and asked that Jesus might abide with him and learn the precepts of the law and all the lessons of the Temple.

20. His parents gave consent, and Jesus did abide in the Temple every day; and every day the master learned from Jesus many lessons of higher life.

21. And the child remained in the Temple of Hillel for a year, and then returned to his home in Nazareth. And there he wrought with Joseph as a carpenter.

Chapter IV
Jesus Talks with the Rabbi of the Ten Commands

1. Now Rabbi Barachia of Nazareth and Jesus, the son of Joseph and Mary met. The Rabbi was aid in teaching the son.

2. One morning after service in the Temple, Jesus, as he sat in silent thought, the Rabbi said to Jesus, "Which is the greatest of the ten commands?"

3. And Jesus said, "I do not see the greatest of the ten commands; I see a gold cord that runs through all the ten commands; that binds them fast and makes them one."

4. "This cord is Love; and it belongs to every word of all the ten commands."

5. "If one is full of Love, he can nothing else but worship Allah; for Allah is Love."

6. And if one is full of Love, he cannot kill; he cannot falsely testify, he cannot covet. He can do naught but honor Allah and man."

7. "If one is full of Love, he does not need commands of any kind."

8. And Rabbi Barachia said, "Your words are seasoned with the salt of wisdom that is from above. Who is the teacher who has opened up this Truth to you?"

9. And Jesus said, "I do not know any teacher opened up this Truth for me. It seems to me that Truth was never shut; that it was always opened up; for Truth is one and it is everywhere."

10. "And, if we open up the windows of our minds, the Truth will enter in and make herself at home; for Truth can find her way through any crevice, any window, any open door."

11. The Rabbi said, "What hand is strong enough to open up the windows and the doors of our minds so Truth can enter in?"

12. And Jesus said, "It seems to me that Love, the golden cord that binds the ten commands in one, is strong enough to open any human door so that Truth can enter in, and cause the heart to understand."

13. Now in the evening Jesus and his mother sat alone; and Jesus said,

14. "The Rabbi seems to think that Allah is partial in his treatments of the sons of men; that Jews are favored and blessed above all other men."

15. "I do not see how Allah can have favorites and be just."

16. "Are not the Samaritans and the Greeks and Romans just as much the children of the Holy One as are the Jews?"

17. "I think the Jews have built a wall about themselves, and they see nothing on the other side of it."

18. "They do not know that flowers are blooming over there; that sowing time belongs to anyone but the Jews."

19. "It surely would be well if we could break these barriers down so that the Jews might see that Allah has other children that are just as greatly blest"

20. "I want to go from Jewry land and meet my kin in other countries of my fatherland."

Chapter V

Jesus Again: His First Year of Divine Ministry

"The Jewish paschal feast time came. And Jesus left His mother in Capernaum, and journeyed to Jerusalem"

1. And he abode with one a Sadducee whose name was Jude.

2. And when he reached the Temple court, the multitudes were there to see the Prophet whom the people thought had come to break the yoke of Rome, and restore the kingdom of the Jews and the rules of David's throne.

3. And when the people saw him come, they said, "All hail."

4. But Jesus answered not. He saw the moneychangers in the house of Allah, and he was grieved.

5. The courts had been converted into marts of trade, and men were selling lambs and doves for the priests.

6. And Jesus called the priest and said, "Behold, for paltry gain, you have sold out the Temple of Allah!"

7. "This house ordained for prayer is now a den of thieves. Can good and evil dwell together in the courts of Allah? I tell you No!"

8. And then he drove them out and over-turned the boards.

9. He opened up the cages of the captive birds, and cut the cords that bound the lambs and set them free.

10. The priests and scribes rushed out; and would have done him harm, but the common people drove them back and stood in his defense.

11. And then the rules said, "Who is this Jesus you can call Divine?"

12. The people said, "He is the one the Prophets wrote concerning, who would come and bring the world the Love of Allah made known to men of earth, who will deliver Israel."

13. The ruler said to Jesus, "If you be the one to come, then show us a sign. Who gave you the right to drive these merchants out?"

14. And Jesus said, "There is no loyal Jew who would not give his life to save this Temple from disgrace. In this, I acted simply as a loyal Jew; and you yourselves will bear me witness to the Truth."

15. "The sign of my Messiahship will follow me in word and deed."

16. "And you may tear the Temple down; and in three days, it will be built again."

17. Now Jesus meant that they might take his life-tear down his body Temple of the Holy Breath, and he would rise again.

18. "You men of Israel, hear! This man is more than man. Take heed to what you do. I have myself heard Jesus speak, and all the winds were still."

19. "And you will see his star arise, and it will grow until it is the full orbed sun of Love."

20. And Jesus said, "Prepare, O Israel, prepare to meet your king; but you can never see the king while you press sin to your hearts."

21. "This king is Allah; the pure in heart alone can see the face of Allah and live."

Chapter VI

Jesus Presented with His Camel, Goes to Lahore Where He Abides

1. A caravan of merchantmen was journeying through the Kasmar vale as Jesus passed that way. And they were going to Lahore, a city of the land, the five-stream land.

2. The merchantmen had heard the Prophet speak; had seen his mighty works in Leh. And they were glad to see him once again.

3. And when they knew that he was going to Lahore, and then across the Sindh through Persia, and further west, and that he had no beast on which to ride.

4. They freely gave to him a noble Bactrian beast, well saddled and equipped. And Jesus journeyed with the caravan.

5. And when he reached Lahore, Ajainin and some other Brahmic priest received him with delight.

6. Ajainin was the priest who came to Jesus in the nighttime in Benares many months before and heard his words of truth.

7. And Jesus was Ajainin's guest. He taught again in many things; revealed to him the secret of the healing art.

8. He taught him how he could control the spirits of the air, the fire, the water and the earth; and explained to him the secret doctrine of forgiveness, and blotting out of sin.

9. One day Ajainin sat with Jesus in the Temple porch. A bank of wandering singers and musicians paused before the court to sing and play.

10. Their music was most rich and delicate; and Jesus said, "Among the high-bred people of the land, we have no sweeter music than these uncouth children of the wilderness bring here to us."

11. "From whence came this talent and this power? In one short life they surely could not gain such grace of voice, such knowledge of the laws of harmony and tone."

12. "These people are not young. A thousand years ago would not suffice to give them such divine expressiveness and such purity of voice and touch."

13. "Men all them prodigies. There are no prodigies. All things result from natural law."

14. "Ten thousand years ago these people mastered harmony. In days of old they trod the busy thorough-fares of life and caught the melody of birds, and played on harps of perfect form."

15. "And they have come again to learn still other lessons from the varied notes of manifests."

16. "These wandering people form a part of heaven's orchestra; and in the land of perfect things, the very angels will delight to hear them play and sing."

17. And Jesus taught the common people of Lahore. He healed their sick, and showed to them the way to rise to better things by helping others.

18. He said, "We are not rich by what we get and hold; the only things we keep are those we give away."

19. "If we would live a perfect life, give forth our life in service for our kind, and for the form of life, that men esteem the lower forms of life."

20. But Jesus could not tarry longer in Lahore. He bade the priest and other friends farewell; and then he took his camel and he went his way towards Sindh.

Chapter VII

Again Elihu's lessons - The Mysteries of Egypt

Again Elihu taught; he said, "The Indian Priests became corrupt; Brahm was forgotten in the streets; the rights of men were trampled in the dust."

1. "And then a mighty master came, a Buddha of enlightenment who turned away from wealth and all honors of the world, and found the silence in the graves and caves; and he was blest."

2. He taught the gospel of higher life, and taught men how to honor man.

3. He had no doctrine of the gods to teach; he just knew man; and so his creed was Justice, Love, and Righteousness.

4. I quote to you a few of many of the helpful words which Buddha spoke.

5. "Hate is a cruel word. If man hates you, regard it not, and you can turn the hate of men to Love, and Mercy and Good Will. Mercy is as large as all the heavens.

6. And there is good enough for all. With good destroy the bad. With generous deeds make avarice ashamed. With Truth make straight the crooked lines that errors draw; for error is but Truth distorted- gone astray.

7. And pain will follow him who speaks or acts with evil thought, as does the wheel the foot of him who draws the cart.

8. He is the greater man who conquers self than he who kills a thousand men in war.

9. He is the noble man who is himself what he believes that other men should be.

10. Return to him who does you wrong your purest love, and he will cease from doing wrong; for love will purify the heart of him who is beloved, as truly as it purifies the heart of him who loves."

11. The words of Buddha are recorded in the Indian sacred books. Attendeth them for they are part of the instructions of the Holy Breath.

12. The land of Egypt is the land of secret things.

13. The mysteries of the sages lie lock-bound in our Temples and Shrines.

14. The masters of all times and climes come here to learn. And when your sons have grown to manhood, they will finish all their studies in Egyptian schools.

15. But I have said enough. Tomorrow at the rising of the sun, we meet again.

Chapter VIII

The Council of the Seven of the World

1. In every age since time began, but seven sages lived.

2. At first of every age these sages meet to note the course of nations, people, tribes and tongues,

3. To note how far towards Justice and love the race has gone;

4. To formulate the ode of law, religious postulates and plans of rule best suited to the coming age.

5. An age had passed, and lo, another age had come. The sages must convene.

6. Now Alexandria was the center of the world's best thought; and here in Philo's home the sages met.

7. From China came Mengste; from India Vidyapati came; from Persia Kasper came; and from Assyria Ashbina came; from Greece Apollo came; Matheno was the Egyptian sage, and Philo was the chief of Hebrew thought.

8. The time was due. The council met and sat in silence seven days.

9. And the Mengste rose and said, "The wheel of time has turned once more. The race is on a higher plane of thought."

10. "The garments that our fathers wore have given out. The cherubim have woven a celestial cloth, have placed it in our hands and we must make for men new garbs."

11. "The sons of men are looking up for greater light. No longer do they care for gods hewn out of wood. They seek for Allah not made with hands."

12. "They see the beams of coming days, and yet comprehend them not."

13. "The time is ripe. And we must fashion well these garments for the race."

14. "And let us make for men new garbs of Justice, Mercy, and Love, that they may hide their nakedness when shines the light of coming days."

15. And Vidyapati said, "Our priests have all gone mad. They saw a demon in the wilds, and at him cast their lamps, and they are broken up, and not a gleam of light has any priest for men."

16. "The night is dark. The heart of India calls for light."

17. "The priesthood cannot be reformed; it is already dead; its greatest needs are graves and funeral chants."

18. "The new age calls for liberty - the kind that makes each man a priest; enables him to go alone and lay his offerings on the Shrine of Allah."

19. And Kaspar said, "In Persia people walk in fear. They do the good for fear to do the wrong."

20. "The devil is the greatest power in our land. And, though a myth, he dandles on his knees both youth and age."

21. "Our land is dark; and evil prospers in the dark."

22. "Fear rides on every passing breeze, and lurks in every form of life."

23. "The fear of evil is a myth; is an illusion and snare; but it will live until some mighty power shall come to raise the ethers to the plane of light."

24. "When this shall come to pass, the Magian land will glory in the light. The soul of Persia calls for Light."

Chapter IX

Opening Address of Jesus with the Seven Sages - Seven Days Silence

1. Ashbina said, "Assyria is the land of doubt. The chariot of my people that in which they mostly ride is labeled, 'DOUBT'".

2. "Once Faith walked in Babylon and she was bright and fair; but she was clothed in such white robes that men became afraid of her."

3. "And every wheel began to turn; and Doubt made war on her and drove her from the land, and she came back no more."

4. "In form man worships Allah, the one; in heart they are not sure that Allah exists."

5. "Faith worships at the Temple of one not seen; but Doubt must see her god."

6. "The greatest need of all Assyria is faith; a faith that seasons everything that is with certainty."

7. And then Apollo said, "The greatest needs of Greece are true conceptions of Allah the one."

8. "In Greece, it is rudderless for every thought may be a god to worship as Allah."

9. "The plane of thought is broad, and full of sharp antagonists. And so the circle of the gods is filled with enmity, with wars and base intrigues."

10. "Greece needs a master-mind to stand above the gods; to raise the mind of men away from many gods to Allah the one."

11. "We know the light is coming over the hills-Allah speed the light."

12. Matheno said, "Behold this land of Egypt of the dead."

13. "Our Temples long have been the tombs of hidden things of time. Our Temple crypts and caves are dark."

14. "In light there is no secret thing. The sun reveals all hidden truth. There are no mysteries in Allah."

15. "Behold the rising sun. His beams are entering every door; yes; every crevice of the mystic crypts of Mizraim."

16. "We hail the light. All Egypt craves the light."

17. And Philo said, "The need of Hebrew thought and life is Liberty."

18. "The Hebrew Prophets, seers and givers of the law were men of power, men of holy thought; and they bequeathed to us a system of love that was ideal; one strong enough to lead our people to the goal of perfectness."

19. "But carnal minds repudiated this law of love, and filled the minds with selfishness. And purity in heart became a myth. The people were enslaved."

20. "But when he comes who is to come, he will proclaim emancipation for the slaves. My people will be free."

21. "Behold, for Allah has made incarnate, wisdom, love and light which he called, Immanuel."

22. "To him is given the key to open up the dawn. And here, as man, he walked with us."

23. And then the council chamber door was opened; and the Logos stood among the sages of the world.

24. Again the sages sat in silence seven days.

Chapter X

Meeting of the Seven Sages to Make Laws for the Coming Age for the Nations of the Earth.

Now when the sages were refreshed, they opened up the book of life and read.

1. They read the story of the life of man; of all his struggles, losses and gains, and in the light of past events and deeds, they saw what would be best for him in coming years.

2. They knew the kind of law and precepts suited to his estate. They saw the highest Allah-Ideal that the race could comprehend.

3. Upon the seven postulates these sages were to formulate the law of life of the coming age that souls may rest.

4. Now Mengste was the oldest sage. He took the chair of chief, and said,

5. "Man is not far enough advanced to live by faith. He cannot comprehend the things his eyes see not."

6. "He yet is child; and during all the coming age must be taught by pictures, symbols, rites and forms."

7. "His God must be a human God. He cannot see Allah by faith."

8. "And he cannot rule himself. The king must rule, the man must serve."

9. "The age that follows this will be the age of man- the age of faith."

10. "In that blest age the human race will see without the aid of carnal eyes; will hear the soundless sound, will know the Spirit-Allah."

11. "The age we enter is the preparation age; and all the schools must be designed in a simple way that men may comprehend."

12. "And man cannot originate. He builds by patterns that he can see. So, in this council, we must carve out patterns for the coming age."

13. "And we must formulate the gnosis of the empire of the soul which rests on seven."

14. "Each sage, in turn, shall form a postulate; and these shall be the basis of the creeds of men until the perfect age shall come."

15. Then Mengste wrote the first.

16. "All things are thought; all life is thought-activity. The multitudes of beings are but phases of the one great thought made manifest. Lo, Allah is thought, and thought is Allah."

17. Then Vidyapati wrote the second postulate.

18. "Eternal thought is one. In essence it is two - intelligence and force; and, when they breathe a child is born; this child is Love."

19. "And thus the Triune Allah stands forth, whom men call father, mother, son."

20. "This Triune Allah is one; but like the one of light, in essence he is seven."

21. "And when the Triune Allah breathes forth, lo, seven spirits stand before his face. These are Creative attributes."

22. "Men call them lesser gods, and in their image they made man."

23. And Kaspar wrote the third.

24. "Man was a thought of Allah formed in the image of the Septonate, clothed in the substance of soul."

25. "And his desires were strong. He sought to manifest on every plane of life. And for himself he made a body of the ethers of the earthy forms; and so he descended to the plane of earth."

26. "In this descent he lost his birth-right, lost his harmony with Allah, made discordant all the notes of life."

27. "Inharmony and evil are the same. So evil is the hand-work of man."

28. Ashbina wrote the fourth.

29. "Seeds do not germinate in light. They do not grow until they find the soil and hide themselves away from light."

30. "Man was evolved a seed of everlasting life; but in the ethers of the Triune Allah, the light was far too great for seeds to grow."

31. "And so man sought the soil of carnal life; and in the darksomeness of earth he found a place where he could germinate and grow."

32. "The seed has taken root and grown full well."

33. "The tree of life is rising from the soil of earthy things, and, under natural law, is reaching up to perfect form."

34. "There are no supernatural acts of Allah to lift a man from carnal life to spirit blessedness. He grows as grows the plant; and, in due time is perfected."

35. "The quality of soul that makes it possible for man to rise to spirit life is purity."

Chapter XI

Jesus Reveals the Marriage Law of Man and Wife from Allah

1. The law forbids adultery; but, in the eyes of the law, adultery is an overt act; the satisfaction of the sensuous self, outside the marriage bonds.

2. Now, marriage, in the sight of the law, is but a promise made by man and woman, by the sanction of the priest, to live together until death.

3. No priest or officer has the power from Allah to bind two souls in wedded Love.

4. What is a marriage tie? It is not what the priest may say or do. There is but one true marriage; and Allah alone can perform this marriage.

5. It is the love of Allah that finds its way into the two - man and woman's hearts; and that is all ever to be. Your priests cannot cause this to be.

6. It is the promise of the two that they will love each other until death.

7. Is love a passion that is subject to the will of man?

8. Can man pick up his love as he would a gem, and lay it down or give it out to anyone?

9. Can love be bought and sold like sheep?

10. Love is the power of Allah that binds two souls and makes them one. There is no power on earth that can dissolve this bond.

11. The bodies may be forced apart by man or death for just a little time, but they will meet again.

12. Now, in this bond of Allah, we find the marriage tie. All other unions are but bonds of straw; and they who live in them commit adultery.

13. But more than this; the man or woman who indulges lustful thoughts commits adultery.

14. Whom Allah has joined together, man cannot part. Whom man has joined together lie in sin.

15. But lo, I say that he who in the heart desires to possess that which is not his own, is a thief in the sight of Allah. The things which men see not with eyes of flesh are of more worth than the thing that men can see.

16. A good name is worth a thousand times a mine of gold; and he who says a word, or does a deed that injures or defames that name is a thief.

17. Upon the table of the law we read, "Thou shalt not covet anything."

18. To covet is an all-consuming wish to have anything that is not right for anyone to have; and such wish in the spirit of the law is theft.

Chapter XII

Jesus Explains to Kaspar the Meaning of Silence and the Wisdom of Allah in Man

1. Now, in the early morning Jesus came again to teach and heal. A light not comprehended shown about as though some mighty spirit overshadowed him.

2. A Magnus noted this and asked him privately to tell from whence his wisdom came, and what is the meaning of the light.

3. And Jesus said, "There is a silence where the soul may meet its God-Allah; and there the fount of wisdom is; and all who enter are immersed in light and filled with wisdom, love and power."

4. The Magnus said, "Tell me about this silence and this light that I may go and there abide."

5. And Jesus said, "The silence is not circumscribed; it is not a place closed in with walls or rocky steeps, nor guarded by the swords of man."

6. "Men carry with them all the time the secret place where they meet Allah."

7. "It matters not where men abide; on mountaintop, in the deep vale, in the marts of trade or in a quiet home, they may at one time fling wide the door of the soul and find the house of Allah. It is within the soul."

8. "One may not be so much disturbed by noise of business and words and thoughts of men it goes all alone into the valley or the mountain pass."

9. "And when life's heavy load is pressing hard, it is far better to go out and seek a quiet place to pray and meditate."

10. "The silence is the kingdom of the soul, which is not seen by human eyes."

11. "When in silence, phantom forms may flit before the mind; but they are all subservient to the will. The master soul may speak, and they are gone."

12. "If you would find this silence of the soul, you must yourself prepare the way. None but the pure in heart may enter here."

13. "And you must lay aside all fears and doubts and troubled thoughts."

14. "Your human will must be absorbed by love divine; then you will come into a consciousness of the Holy Breath."

15. "You are within a holy place, and you will see upon a living shrine the candle of Allah aflame."

16. "And when you see it burning there, look deep within the Temple of your brain; you will see it all aglow."

17. "In every part from head to foot are candles all in place, just waiting to be lighted by the flaming torch of Love."

18. "And when you see the candles all aflame, just look and you will see, with eyes of soul, the waters of the fount of wisdom rushing on; and you may drink and there abide."

19. "And the curtains part; and you are where the Ark of Allah rests, whose covering is the mercy seat."

20. "Fear not to lift the sacred board; the tables of the law are in the Ark concealed."

21. "Take them and read them well; for they contain all the precepts that man will ever need."

22. "And in the Ark the magic wand, for they contain all prophecy, lies waiting for our hands. It is the key to all the hidden meanings of present, future and past."

23. "The Cherubim have guarded well for every soul this treasure box; and whosoever will may enter in and find his own."

24. Now Kaspar heard the Hebrew master speak and he exclaimed, "Behold, the wisdom of Allah has come to men."

25. And Jesus went his way, and in the sacred grove of Cyrus was met. He taught and healed the sick.

Chapter XIII

Jesus's Holy Answer to Lamaas

1. Now, after they had dined, the guests and Jesus all were in a spacious hall in Mary's home.

2. And Lamaas said, "Pray tell us, Jesus, is this the dawn of peace?"

3. "Have we come forth unto the time when men will war no more?"

4. "Are you indeed the prince of peace that holy men have said would come?"

5. And Jesus said, "Peace reigns today; it is the peace of death."

6. "A stagnant pool abides in peace. When waters cease to move they soon are laden with the seeds of death. Corruption dwells in every drop."

7. "The living waters always leap and skip about like lambs in spring."

8. "The nations are corrupt. They sleep within the arms of death, and they must be aroused before it is too late."

9. "In life we find antagonists at work. Allah sent me here to stir unto its depths the waters of the sea of life."

10. "Peace follows strife. I come to slay this peace of earth. The prince of peace must first be prince of strife."

11. "This leaven of truth which I have brought to men will stir the demons up, and nations, cities, families will be at peace with themselves."

12. "The five that have been dwelling in a home in peace will be divided not; and two shall war against three."

13. "The son will stand against his sire; the mother and daughter will contend. Yea; strife will reign in every home."

14. "Then self and greed and doubt will rage into a fever heat. And then, because of me, the earth will be baptized in human blood."

15. "But right is king; and when the smoke is cleared away, the nations will learn war no more. The prince of peace will come to reign.

16. "Behold, the signs of what I say are in the sky, but men can see them not."

17. "When men behold a cloud rise in the west they say a shower of rain will come; and so it does. And when the wind blows from the south, they say the weather will be hot; and it is so"

18. "Lo, men can read the signs of earth and sky, but they cannot discern the signs of the Holy Breath; but you shall know."

19. "The storms of wrath come on. The carnal man will seek a cause to hale you into court, and cast you into prison cells."

20. "And, when these times shall come, let wisdom guide; do not resent. Resentment makes more strong the wrath of evil men."

21. "There is a little sense of Justice and of Mercy in the vilest men of earth."

22. "By taking heed to what you do and say, and trusting in the guidance of the Holy Breath, you may inspire this sense to grow."

23. "You thus may make the wrath of men to praise Allah."

24. And Jesus went his way and came unto Bethsada and taught.

Chapter XIV

Jesus Receives the Mystic Name and Number and Passed the First Brother-hood Test

The master took down from the wall a scroll on which was written down the number and name of every attribute, character; and he said.

1. "The Circle is the symbol of the perfect man; and the Seven is the number of the perfect man."
2. "The Logos is the perfect word; that which creates, that which destroys, and that which saves."
3. "This Hebrew master is the Logos of the Holy One, the Circle of the human race, the Seven of the time."
4. And in the record book, the scribe wrote down, "The Logos, Circle, Seven," and thus was Jesus known.
5. The master said, "The Logos will give heed to what I say. No man can enter into light till he has found himself; go forth and search till you have found your soul and then return."
6. The guide led Jesus to a room in which the light was faint and mellow like the light of early dawn.
7. The chamber walls were marked with mystic signs, with hieroglyphs and sacred texts; and in the chamber Jesus found himself alone where he remained for many days.
8. He read the sacred texts, thought out the meanings of the hieroglyphs and sought the import of the master's charge to find himself.
9. A revelation came. He got acquainted with his soul. He found himself; then he was not alone.

10. One night he slept, and at midnight hour a door that he had not observed was opened and a priest in somber garb came in and said,

11. "My brother, pardon me for coming in at this unseemly hour; but I have come to save your life."

12. "You are the victim of a cruel plot. The priests of Heliopolis are jealous of your fame, and they have said that you will never leave these gloomy crypts alive."

13. "The higher priests do not go forth to teach the world; and you are doomed to Temple servitude."

14. "Now, if you would be free, you must deceive these priests; must tell them you are here to stay for life."

15. "And then you will have gained all that you wish to gain, I will return; and, by a secret way, will lead you forth that you may go in peace."

16. And Jesus said, "My brother man, would you come here to teach deceit? Am I within these holy walls to learn the wiles of vile hypocrisy?"

17. "Nay, man; my father scorns deceit; and I am here to do Hi will."

18. "Deceive these priests? Not while the sun shines! What I have said I have said. I will be true to them, to Allah and to myself."

19. And then the tempter left, and Jesus was again alone; but in a little time a white-robed priest appeared and said,

20. "Well done. The Logos has prevailed. This is the trial chamber of hypocrisy." And then he led the way, and Jesus stood before the judgment seat.

21. And all the brothers stood. The hierophant came forth and laid hands on Jesus's head and placed within his hand a scroll on which was written just one word; "SINCERITY". And not a word was said.

22. The guide again appeared and led the way, in the spacious room replete with everything a student craves, was Jesus bade to rest and wait.

Chapter XV

Jesus Passes the Second Brother-hood Test - Justice

The Logos did not care to rest. He said, "Why wait in this luxurious room? I need not rest; my father's work upon me presses hard."

1. "I would go on and learn my lessons all. If there are trials, let them come; for every victory over self gives added strength."

2. And then the guide led on. And in a chamber dark as night was Jesus placed and left alone. And days were spent in this deep solitude.

3. And Jesus slept; and in the dead of the night, a secret door was opened, and in priest's attire two men came in, each carrying in his hand a little flickering lamp.

4. Approaching Jesus, one spoke out and said, "Young man, our hearts are grieved because of what you suffer in these fearful dens, and we have come as friends to bring you light and show the way to liberty."

5. "We, once like you were in these dens confined, and thought that through these weird, uncanny ways we could attain to blessedness and power;"

6. "But, in a luckful moment, we were undeceived, and making use of all our strength, we broke our chains; and then we learned that all this service is corruption in disguise. These priests are criminals just hid away."

7. "They boast of sacrificial rites; they offer to their gods, and burn them while alive, poor birds and beasts; yea children, women and men."

8. And now they keep you here; and at a certain time, may offer you in sacrifice.

9. We pray you brother, break your chains. Come go with us; accept of freedom while you may."

10. And Jesus said. "Your little tapers show the light you bring. Pray, who are you? The words of man are worth no more than is the man himself."

11. "These Temple walls are strong and high; how gained you entrance to this place?"

12. The men replied, "Beneath these walls are hidden ways and we who have been priests spent months and years within these dens and know all of them"

13. "Then you are traitors!" Jesus said; "A traitor is a friend who betrays another man, is never a man to trust."

14. "If one has only reached the plane of treachery, he is a lover of deceit, and will betray a friend to save his selfish self."

15. "Behold, you men, or whatsoever you be, your words fall lightly on my ears."

16. "Could I prejudge these hundred priests, turn traitor to myself and them, because of what you say, when you confess your treachery?"

17. "No man can judge for me; and if I judge before testimony all is in, I might not judge aright."

18. "Nay, men; by whatsoever way you came, return. My soul prefers the darkness of the grave to little flickering light like these you bring."

19. "My conscience rules. What these, my brothers have to say, I will hear; and, when the testimony all is in, I will decide. You cannot judge for me, nor I for you."

20. "Be gone! You men, be gone! And leave to me this charming light; for, while the sun shines not, within my soul there is a light surpassing that of sun and moon!"

21. Then, with an angry threat that they would do him harm, the vile tempters left; and Jesus was alone.

22. Again the white-robed priest appeared and led the way; and Jesus stood again before the hierophant.

23. And not a word was said; but in his hands the master placed as scroll on which the word "JUSTICE" was inscribed.

24. And Jesus was the master of the phantom forms of prejudice and of treachery.

Chapter XVI
Jesus Passes the Third Brother-hood Test - FAITH

The Logos waited seven days; and then was taken to the Hall of Fame, a chamber rich in furnishings, and lighted up with gold and silver lamps.

1. The colors of its ceiling decorations, furnishing and walls were blue and gold.

2. Its shelves were filled with books of masterminds. The paintings and the statues were the works of highest art.

3. And Jesus was entranced with all this elegance and these manifests of thought. He read the sacred books, and sought the meaning of the symbols and the hieroglyphs.

4. And when he was absorbed in deepest thought, a priest approached and said,

5. "Behold the glory of this place! My brother you are blest. Few men of earth so young have reached such heights of fame."

6. "Now, if you do not waste your life in search for hidden things that man can never comprehend, you may be founder of a school of thought that will assure you endless fame."

7. "For your philosophy is deeper far than that of Plato; and your teachings please the common people more than those of Socrates."

8. "Why seek for mystic light within these antiquated dens? Go forth and walk with men, and they will honor you."

9. "And, after all, these weird initiations may be myths; and your messiah hopes but illusions of the hour."

10. "I would advise you to renounce uncertain things, and choose the course that leads to certain fame."

11. And thus, the priest - a demon in disguise - sang siren songs of unbelief. And Jesus meditated long and well on what he said.

12. The conflict was a bitter one; for king ambition is a sturdy foe to fight.

13. For forty days the higher self wrestled with the lower self. And then the fight was on.

14. FAITH rose triumphant; unbelief was not; ambition covered up his face and fled away. And Jesus said,

15. "The wealth, the honor and the fame of earth are but the baubles of the hour."

16. When this short span of earthly life has been measured out, man's bursting baubles will be buried with his bones.

17. "Yes; what man does for his selfish self will make no markings on the credit side of life."

18. "The good that man for other men shall do, becomes a ladder strong, on which the soul may climb to wealth and power and fame of Allah's own kind that cannot pass away."

19. "Give me the poverty of men; the consciousness of duty done in love; the approbation of Allah, and I will be content."

20. And he lifted up his eyes to heaven, and said,

21. "My Father Allah, I thank thee for this hour. I ask not for the glory of myself; I fain would be a keeper of the Temple gates, and serve my brother-man."

22. Again was Jesus called to stand before the hierophant. Again no word was said; but in his hands the master placed a scroll on which was written, "FAITH".

23. And Jesus bowed his head in humble thanks and went his way.

Chapter XVII

Jesus Passes the Fourth Brother-hood Test; Takes the Fourth Degree of Adept

Whether other certain days had passed, the guide led Jesus to the hall of mirth; a hall most richly furnished, and replace with everything a carnal heart could wish.

1. The choicest viands and most delicious wines were on the boards. And maids in gay attire served all with grace and cheerfulness.

2. And men and women richly clad were there. And they were wild with joy. They sipped from cheery cups of mirth.

3. And Jesus watched the happy throng in silence for a time; and then a man in garb of sage came up and said, "Most happy is the man who, like the bee, can gather sweets from every flower."

4. "The wise man is the one who seeks for pleasure, and can find it everywhere."

5. "At best, man's life on earth is short. And then he dies and goes he knows not where."

6. "Then let us eat and drink and dance and sing; let us get joy of life, for death comes apace."

7. "It is but foolishness to spend a life for other men. Behold, I die and lie together in the grave where none can know, and none can show forth gratitude."

8. But Jesus answered not. Upon the tinseled guests, in all their rounds of mirth, he gazed in silent thought.

9. And then among the guests, he saw a man whose clothes were coarse, who showed in face and hand, the lines of toil and want.

10. The giddy throng found pleasure in abusing him. They jostled him against the walls and laughed at this discomfiture.

11. And a poor frail woman came, who carried in her face and form, the marks of sin and shame. And, without mercy, she was spit upon.

12. And a little child, with timid ways and hungry men came in and asked for just a morsel of their food.

13. But she was driven out uncared for and unloved; and still the merry dance went on.

14. And when the pleasure-seekers urged that Jesus join them in their mirth, he said,

15. "How could I seek for pleasure for myself while others are in want? How can I think that, while the children cry for bread, while those in haunts of sin call out for sympathy and love, that I can fill myself too full with the good things of life?"

16. "I tell you, nay! We all are kin, each one a part of the great human heart."

17. "I cannot see myself apart from that poor man who you so scorned and crowded to the wall."

18. "Nor from the one in female garb, who came up from the haunts of vice to ask for sympathy and love; and who, by you, was so ruthlessly pushed back into her den of sin."

19. "Nor from that little child you drive from your midst to suffer in the cold, bleak winds of night."
20. "I tell you, men; what you have done to them, my kindred, you have done to me."
21. "You have insulted me in your own home. I cannot stay. I will go forth and find that child, that woman and that man, and give them help until my life's blood all has ebbed away."
22. "I will call it pleasure when I help the helpless, feed the hungry, clothe the naked, heal the sick, and speak good words of cheer to those unloved, discouraged, and depressed."
23. "And this that you call mirth is but a phantom of the night; but flashes of the fire of passion painting pictures on the walls of time."
24. And while the Logos spoke the white-robed priest came in and said to him. "The council waits for you."
25. Then, Jesus stood again before the bar. Again no word was said. The hierophant placed in his hand a scroll on which was written, "PHILANTHROPY".
26. And Jesus was a victor over selfish self.

Chapter XVIII
Jesus Passes the Fifth Adept Degree - Heroism

1. The sacred Temple groves were rich in statues, monuments and shrines; here Jesus loved to walk and meditate.
2. And after he had conquered self, he talked with nature in these groves for forty days.
3. And then the guide took chains and bound him hand and foot, and cast him into a den of hungry beasts, of unclean birds and creeping things.

4. The den was dark as night. The wild beasts howled; the birds, in fury, screamed, the reptiles hissed.

5. And Jesus said, "Who is it that did bind me thus? Why did I meekly sit to be bound down with chains?

6. "I tell you, none has power to bind the human soul. Of what are fetters made?"

7. And in his might, he rose; and what he thought were chains were only worthless cords, that parted at his touch.

8. And then he laughed and said, "The chains that bind men to the caracasses of earth are forged in fancy's shop; are made of air and welded in illusion's fires."

9. "If man will stand and use the power of will, his chains will fall like worthless rags; for will and faith are stronger than the stoutest chains that men have ever made."

10. And Jesus stood erect among the hungry beasts and birds and said, "What is this darkness that envelopes me?"

11. "'Tis but the absence of the light. And what is light? 'Tis but the breath of Allah vibrating in the rhythm of rapid thought."

12. And then he said, "Let there be light!" And, with a mighty will, he stirred the ethers up, and their vibrations reached the plane of light; and there was light.

13. The darkness of that den of night became the brightness of a new-born day.

14. And then he looked to see the beasts and birds and creeping things. Lo, they were not.

15. And Jesus said, "Of what is soul afraid? Fear is the chariot in which man rides to death!"

16. "And when he finds himself within the chamber of the dead, he learns that he has been deceived; his chariot was a myth, and death a fancy child."

17. But some day all men's lessons will be learned. And from the den of unclean beasts and birds and creeping things, he will rise to walk in light."

18. And Jesus saw a ladder made of gold, on which he climbed; and at the top the white-robed priest awaited him.

19. Again he stood before the council bar. Again no word was said. Again the hierophant reached for his hand to bless.

20. He placed in Jesus's hand another scroll. And on this one was written "HEROISM".

21. The Logos had encountered fear and all his phantom hosts; and, in the conflict, he achieved the victory.

Chapter XIX

Jesus Takes the Sixth Degree and Passed the Sixth Adept Chamber of the Eastern Sages.

In all the land there was no place more grandly furnished than the beauty parlors of the Temple of the Sun.

1. Few students ever entered these rooms. The priests guarded them with awe, and called them halls of mysteries.

2. When Jesus had attained the victory over fear, he gained the right to enter here.

3. The guide led on the way. And, after passing many richly furnished rooms, they reached the hall of harmony, and there was Jesus left alone.

4. Among the instruments of music was a harpsichord. And Jesus sat in thoughtful mood, inspecting it, when quietly a maiden of entrancing beauty came into the hall.

5. She did not seem to notice Jesus as he sat and mused so busy with his thoughts.

6. She found her place beside the harpsichord. She touched the chords most gently, and she sang the songs of Israel.

7. And Jesus was entranced; such beauty he had never seen, such music he had never heard.

8. The maiden sang her songs. She didn't seem to know that any one was near. She went her way.

9. And Jesus, talking with himself, said out, "What is the meaning of this incident? I did not know that such entrancing beauty and such queen-like loveliness were ever found among the sons of men."

10. "I did not know that voice of angels ever graced a human form; or that seraphic music ever came from human lips."

11. For days he sat entranced. The current of his thoughts was changed. He thought of nothing but the singer and her songs.

12. He longed to see her once again and, after days, she came. She spoke and laid her hand upon his head.

13. Her touch thrilled all his soul; and, for a time, he forgot the work that he was sent to do.

14. Few were the words the maiden said. She went her way; but then the heart of Jesus had been touched.

15. A love-flame had been kindled in his soul, and he was brought to face the sorest trial of life.

16. He could not sleep, nor could he eat. The thoughts of the maiden came; they would not go. His carnal nature called aloud for her companionship.

17. And then, he said, "Lo, I have conquered every foe that I have met, and shall I now be conquered by carnal love?"

18. "My Father sent me her to show the power of love-divine; that love that reaches every living thing."

19. "Shall this pure universal love be all absorbed by carnal love? Shall I forget all creatures else, and lose my life in this fair maiden? Though she is the highest type of beauty, purity and love."

20. Into its very depths, his soul was stirred; and long he wrestled with this angel-idol of his heart.

21. But when the day was almost lost his higher-ego rose in might. He found himself again, and then he said,

22. "Although my heart shall break, I will not fail in this my hardest task. I will be victor over carnal love."

23. And when again the maiden came and offered him her hand and heart, he said,

24. "Fair one, your very presence thrills me with delight. Your voice is benediction to my soul. My human self would fly with you, and be contented in your love."

25. "But all the world is craving for a love that I have come to manifest."

26. "I must then, bid you go, but we will meet again. Our ways on earth will not be cast apart."

27. "I see you in the hurrying throngs of earth as minister of love. I hear your voice in song that wins the hearts of men to better things."

28. And then in sorry and in tears the maiden went away; and Jesus was alone again.

29. Instantly the great bells of the Temple rang. The grotto blazed with light.

30. The hierophant himself appeared, and said, "All hail triumphant Logos; Hail the conqueror of carnal love stands on the height."

31. And then he placed in Jesus's hand a scroll on which was written, "LOVE DIVINE"

32. Together they passed from the grotto of the beautiful Temple, and in the banquet hall a feast was served, and Jesus was the honored guest.

Chapter XX

The Adept Chamber of the Dead. The Mysteries of Egypt.

The senior course of study now was opened up. And Jesus entered and became a pupil of the hierophant.

1. He learned the secrets of the mystic lore of Egyptland, the mysteries of life and death and of the world beyond the circle of the sun.

2. When he had finished all the studies of the senior course, he went into the chamber of the dead that he might learn the ancient methods of preserving from decay, the bodies of the dead, and here he wrought.

3. And carriers brought the body of a widow's son to be embalmed. The weeping mother followed close. Her grief was great.

4. And Jesus said, "Good woman, dry your tears. You follow but an empty house. Your son is in it not."

5. "You weep because your son is dead. Death is not a cruel word. Your son can never die."

6. "He had a task assigned to do in garb of flesh. He came; he did his work; and then he laid the flesh aside; he did not need it more."

7. "Beyond the human sight, he has another work to do, and he will do it well and then pass to other tasks. And by and by he will attain the crown of perfect life."

8. "And what your son has done, and what he yet must do, we all must do."

9. "Now, if you harbor grief and give your sorrows vent, they will grow greater every day. They will absorb your very life until at last you will be naught, we drown with bitter tears."

10. "Instead of helping him, you grieve your son by your deep grief. He seeks your solace now as he has ever done; is glad when you are glad, is saddened when you grieve."

11. "Go bury deep your woes, and smile at grief; and lose yourself in helping others dry their tears."

12. "With duty done comes happiness and joy. And gladness cheers the hearts of those who have passed on."

13. The weeping woman turned and went her way to find happiness in helpfulness; to bury deep her sorrows in a ministry of joy.

14. Then other carriers came and brought the body of a mother to the chamber of the dead. And just one mourner followed, she, a girl of tender years.

15. And as the cortege neared the door, the child observed a wounded bird in sore distress. A cruel hunter's dart had pierced its breast.

16. And she left following the dead, and went to help the living bird.

17. With tenderness and love she folded to her breast the wounded bird, then hurried to her place.

18. And Jesus said to her, "Why did you leave your dead to save a wounded bird?"

19. The maiden said, "This lifeless body needs no help from me. My mother taught me this."

20. "My mother taught that grief and selfish love and hopes and fears are but reflexes from the lower self."

21. "That what we sense is but small waves upon the rolling billows of a life."

22. "These all will pass away. They are unreal."

23. "Tears flow from hearts of flesh. The spirit never weeps; and I am longing of the day when I can walk in the light where tears are wiped away."

24. "My mother taught that all emotions are sprays that rise from human love and hope and fears; that perfect bliss cannot be ours till we have conquered these."

25. And in the presence of that child did Jesus bow his head in reverence. He said,

26. "For days and months and years I have sought to learn this highest truth that man can learn on earth; and here a child, fresh brought to earth, has told it all in one short breath."

27. "No wonder David said, Oh Allah, our Lord; how excellent is thy name in all the earth!"

28. "Out of the mouth of babes and sucklings hast thou ordained strength."

29. And then he laid his hand upon the maiden's head and said, "I am sure the blessings of my Father Allah will rest upon you, Child, forever."

Chapter XXI

Jesus, The Prophet Had Finished His Tasks, and Must Now Go to the Sons of Men with Love Divine and Peace on Earth

The work of Jesus was done; and now he must go to teach the sons of men. And in the Temple he stood and said, "The son of man has come to bring the light - the light of life."

1. And all the brothers stood and said, "This is a royal day for all the hosts of the earth; for salvation has come to all the children of men. Six times before the bar, six times a conqueror."

2. And then one said to Jesus, "Brother-man, most excellent of men, in all the Temple tests you have won out."

3. "Upon your brow I place this diadem; and in the great assembly of all the world and heaven, you are the mastermind of all."

4. "Now man can do no more; but Allah himself will speak and confirm your title. Go your way and teach peace on earth, good will to man."

5. And while the hierophant yet spoke the Temple bells rang out in love; and the Logos journeyed on his way, a conqueror.

Chapter XXII

Jesus Addresses the Seven Sages - Goes to Galilee

1. The seven days of silence passed. And Jesus, sitting with the sages said,

2. "The history of life is well condensed in these immortal postulates. These are the seven hills on which the Holy City shall be built. These are the seven sure foundation stones on which the Temple shall stand."

3. "In taking up the work assigned for me to do, I am full conscious of the perils of the way. The cup will be a bitter one to drink; and human nature well might shrink."

4. "But I have lost my will in that of Holy Breath. And so I go my way to speak and act as I am moved to speak and act by the Holy Breath."

5. "The words I speak are not my own; they are the words of Him whose will I do."

6. "Man is not far enough advanced in sacred thought to comprehend within the Temple of Allah; so the work that Allah gave me to do is to teach men to build the Temple of Love within."

7. "I am sent to be a pattern of the Temple that man must build within."

8. "My task as builder lies within my native land. And there upon was the Temple of might Allah made known - the Allah in man."

9. "And from the lower estate of men, I will select seven men who will represent the Temple of Love - Allah in man."

10. "The house of Judah, my own kindred in flesh, will comprehend but little of my mission to the world;"

11. "And they will spurn me, scorn my work, accuse me falsely, bid me, take me to the judgment seat of carnal men who will convict and slay me."

12. "But man can never slay the truth. Though banished it will come again, in greater power; for truth will subjugate the world."

13. "The Temple will live, though carnal men will prostitute its sacred laws, symbolic rites and forms for selfish ends; and make it but outward show. The few will find through it the kingdom of the soul."

14. "And when the better age shall come, the Temple will stand upon the seven postulates, and will be built according to the pattern given."

15. "The time has come. I go my way unto the world; and, by the power of living faith, and by the strength that you give me."

16. "And in the name of our God-Allah, the kingdom of soul shall be established and seven hills." And all the sages said, "Amen", and Jesus went his way.

Chapter XXIII

Jesus Received the News of His Father's Death. Writes a Letter to His Mother

One day as Jesus stood beside the Ganges busy with his work; a caravan returning from the west drew near.

1. And one approaching Jesus said, "We come to you just from your native land, and bring you welcome news."

2. "Your father is no more on earth; your mother grieves; and none can comfort her. She wonders whether you are still alive or not. She longs to see you once again."

3. And Jesus bowed his head in silent thought. And then he wrote; of what he wrote, this is the sum:

4. "My mother, noblest of woman kind, a man just from my native land has brought me word."

5. "My mother, all is well. Is well for father, is well for you."

6. "His work in this earth-round is done; and it is nobly done."

7. "In all the walks of life, men cannot charge him with deceit, dishonesty, nor wrong intent."

8. "Here in this round, he finished man heavy tasks; and he has gone hence, prepared to solve the problems of the round of soul."

9. "Our Father Allah is with him there as he was with him here. And there his angel guards his footsteps, lest he goes astray."

10. "Why should you weep? Tears cannot conquer grief. There is no power in grief to mend a broken heart."

11. "The plane of grief is idleness. The busy soul can never grieve; it has no time for grief."

12. "When grief comes trooping through the heart, just lose yourself, and plunge deep into the ministry of love, and grief is not."

13. "Yours is a ministry of love; and all the world is calling out for love."

14. "Then let the past go with the past. Rise from cares of carnal things and give your life for those who live."

15. "And if you lose your life in serving life, you will be sure to find it in the morning sun, the evening dew, in songs of birds, in flowers and in the stars of night."

16. "In just a little while our problems of earth-round will be solved; and, when your sums are all worked, it will be pleasure unalloyed for you to enter wider fields of usefulness, to solve the greater problems of the soul."

17. "Strive, then, to be content; and I will come to you some day and bring you richer gifts of gold or precious stones."

18. "I am sure that John will care for you; supplying all your needs. And I am with you always."

Signed,

Jehoshua

19. And by the hands of one, a merchant going to Jerusalem, he sent this letter on its way.

www.ingramcontent.com/pod-product-compliance
Lightning Source LLC
Chambersburg PA
CBHW060343080526
44584CB00013B/904